Napoleon Bonaparte

by Jan Goldberg

Napoleon Bonaparte
by Jan Goldberg

Illustrations by Burgandy Beam

Photography: p. 1 © Francis G. Mayer/CORBIS; p. 3 © Paul Almasy/CORBIS; p. 6 © Bettmann/CORBIS; p. 10 © Christie's Images/CORBIS; p. 13 © Archivo Iconografico, S.A./CORBIS; p. 16 © Bettmann/CORBIS; p. 19 © Archivo Iconografico, S.A./CORBIS; p. 21 © Bettmann/CORBIS; p. 24 © Bettmann/CORBIS; p. 32 © Bettmann/CORBIS; p. 33 © Historical Picture Archive/CORBIS; p. 35 © Bettmann/CORBIS; p. 38 © Gianni Dagli Orti/CORBIS; p. 39 © Bettmann/CORBIS; p. 41 © Archivo Iconografico, S.A./CORBIS; p. 43 © Bettmann/CORBIS; p. 46 © Bettmann/CORBIS; p. 55 © Stapleton Collection/CORBIS; p. 56 © Bill Ross/CORBIS; p. 57 © Bettmann/CORBIS; p. 58 © Bettmann/CORBIS; p. 60 © Burstein Collection/CORBIS; p. 65 © Christie's Images/CORBIS; p. 68 © Bettmann/CORBIS; p. 77 © Bettmann/CORBIS; p. 81 © Bettmann/CORBIS

Nonfiction Reviewer
John Barell, Ed.D.
Educational Consultant, The American Museum of Natural History
New York City

Art Buying by Inkwell Publishing Solutions, Inc., New York City
Cover Design by Inkwell Publishing Solutions, Inc., New York City

ISBN: 0-7367-1799-4

Copyright © Zaner-Bloser, Inc.

All rights reserved. No part of this book may be reproduced or transmitted in any form or by any means, electronic or mechanical, including photocopying, recording, or by any information storage and retrieval system, without permission in writing from the Publisher.

Web sites have been carefully researched for accuracy, content, and appropriateness. However, Web sites are subject to change. Internet usage should always be monitored.

Zaner-Bloser, Inc., P.O. Box 16764, Columbus, Ohio 43216-6764, 1-800-421-3018

Printed in China

03   04   05   06   07   (321)   5   4   3   2   1

TABLE OF CONTENTS

Introduction 1
Chapter One: Young Napoleon 2
Chapter Two: Class Rebellion in France 9
Chapter Three:
   Napoleon Begins His Military Career 15
Chapter Four: Napoleon Comes Into Power 24
Chapter Five: Napoleon as First Consul 36
Chapter Six: Napoleon, Emperor of France 45
Chapter Seven: An End and a New Beginning 54
Chapter Eight: Napoleon Meets His Waterloo 69
Glossary 83
Index 85

INTRODUCTION

Many applaud Napoleon Bonaparte for his accomplishments. Others find fault with some of his actions. For nearly 200 years, he has been both criticized and praised. However, one thing historians agree on is that Napoleon changed the world.

While it is true that Napoleon was not always very nice, he was responsible for a number of positive things. For instance, he created a public school system in France. He also promoted a more efficient government and better laws. Many people believe his greatest achievement was the establishment of the Code Napoleon. It brought fair and equal laws to all citizens of France. Even today, this code is still used in many countries around the world as the basis for their laws.

Napoleon also promoted a feeling of nationalism. Another word for nationalism is *patriotism*. It means that you show pride for your country. When we salute the flag, sing the national anthem, or vote in an election, we are showing our nationalism. Nationalism soon spread throughout Europe and then to the rest of the world.

Napoleon was incredibly tough and he showed a great deal of courage, both in victory and in defeat. He dared to rule Europe and in the process, he made a name for himself in history.

CHAPTER ONE

Young Napoleon

Napoleon was born on the island of Corsica (**kor**•si•kuh) on August 15, 1769, in a village named Ajaccio (ah•**yah**•choh). This island, the fourth largest in the Mediterranean Sea, is about the size of the state of Louisiana. It lies about 100 miles west of Italy and a little more than 100 miles (161 kilometers) southeast of France. Corsica belonged to Italy for hundreds of years, until 1768. That is the year when France bought all

Ajaccio, Corsica

rights to the island. Even though Napoleon was born on Corsica, he technically was a citizen of France.

At the time of Napoleon's birth, the French felt that the citizens of Corsica were wild and rebellious. They were also very poor. Napoleon was embarrassed to be Corsican. So, he changed the original spelling of his first and last names. He thought "Napoleone Buonaparte" looked and sounded too Italian, or too Corsican. He wanted to be thought of as a Frenchman. He became "Napoleon Bonaparte."

Did You Know?

In Ajaccio, Corsica, the Buonaparte family lived in a large, four-story house. Napoleon's parents lived in the house for a long time. Napoleon and all of his brothers and sisters, except Joseph, were born there.

One legend says that Napoleon's mother gave birth to him on the floor on a worn-out rug. It is also said that this rug was decorated with heroic war scenes from a book called *The Iliad*. It is the story of an ancient war between the Greeks and the Trojans. Those who believed the legend said that it meant Napoleon would be a great military leader. However, it is unlikely that the story is true. The Buonaparte home was not fancy enough to have expensive furnishings like decorated rugs. And if their home did have rugs, they would have been put away for the hot summer months.

Famous Name Changers

Many people throughout history have changed their first name, last name, or both. Some make the change for the same reason that Napoleon did. Many keep a similar name but change it only slightly or change the spelling.

Remember Paul Revere? The famous patriot rode his horse through Boston so he could warn his fellow colonists that "The British are coming!" Paul Revere's father changed Paul's name when he was young because he wanted his son to have a name that was easier to pronounce. His original name was Apollos Rivoire.

Some people change their name to something completely different. Their new name doesn't sound anything like their old name. Many movie stars and musicians take new names as "stage names." They decide that they want a name that sounds better, is easier to pronounce, is easier to spell, or is easier to remember. This is why Reginald Dwight changed his name to Elton John. The actress who played Dorothy in *The Wizard of Oz* changed her name from Ethel Gumm to Judy Garland.

Napoleon's Family

Napoleon's parents were Carlo and Letizia Ramolino (leh•**teet**•zee•uh rah•moh•**lee**•noh) de Buonaparte. Napoleon was their fourth child and their second son. His parents had thirteen children in all. Only eight of them lived past infancy.

Napoleon had three sisters and four brothers. Like Napoleon, all of his siblings held positions in politics or as royalty. But none were as successful as Napoleon.

The Corsican Revolution

Napoleon's father was a lawyer on Corsica. He had a higher social rank on the island than most people did. But this did not mean that he had any power or that he was rich. In fact, the Buonaparte family was quite poor. Many of Carlo's clients could not afford to pay him money. He was often offered goods and services instead.

Carlo and Letizia did not want their island to be under the rule of France. They joined the Corsican **revolution** led by a man named Pasquale Paoli (pahs•**kwah**•lay pah•**oh**•lee). Those who joined the revolution were fighting for Corsican freedom from the French. Being a part of the revolution was difficult for the Buonaparte family. It was especially difficult for the young children. The family moved around Corsica to escape the French who had come to stop the revolution. The family had to stay in camps that were dirty and uncomfortable. They were often hungry. Sometimes they were forced to hide out in cold and dark caves. Many other members of the Buonaparte family were also involved in the fight against the French. In fact, Napoleon was named after his cousin Napoleone, who died in early 1769 while fighting for Corsican independence.

After several years of fighting for Corsica, Napoleon's father realized that his family was suffering. He decided he could not be a part of the revolution anymore. He got a job working for the Corsican government. The position gave him more money to support his growing family. After a while, he had enough power to enroll Napoleon in a private school called a *preparatory school*. The school was located in Autun (oh•**tun**), France.

Educating Young Napoleon

Napoleon was only nine years old when he left for France to go to the private school in Autun. The other boys at the school laughed at him because he was much shorter than the rest of the class. They also made fun of his Corsican accent. Their teasing gave Napoleon the determination to succeed. Napoleon was determined to improve upon how to speak French. Eventually he was able to speak it as well as his other classmates.

After a few months at the school in Autun, Napoleon's father got his son a scholarship to attend a different school in France. This time, he went to an important military academy called *Brienne-le-Château*. Attending military school changed Napoleon's life forever. It was here that he learned about war. It was here that he began to believe that he was meant to live a military life.

Napoleon was teased by his classmates.

After five years of military training, the school decided Napoleon would make an excellent sailor. They recommended he join the French navy. Napoleon disagreed. He thought that he could have a more important military career if he joined the army instead. To do so, he must attend military college. In 1784, he was chosen to attend France's most **prestigious** military college, the École Militaire (ay•**kohl** mee•lee•**tair**) in Paris.

Napoleon rushed through his studies at the military college. It took him only a year to complete the program, while most other students required two years to complete the same amount of schoolwork. Napoleon was determined to get his military career started quickly.

When he was only sixteen years old, Napoleon was given the title of second lieutenant in the artillery. The artillery was the branch of the French army that specialized in large mounted guns, like cannons. During a war, the artillery unit would be responsible for the operation of these types of weapons. Napoleon was part of a regiment, or military unit, called the *Régiment de la Fère* (ray•zhee•**mahn** duh lah **fair**), at Valence (vah•**lahns**), France.

Napoleon did not lead a military life right away because France was not involved in any military action at the time. He only took part in military training exercises occasionally.

Did You Know?

Napoleon was only 5'6" (1.67 meters) tall. Because he was so short and so brave, he got the nickname of "le Petit Caporal." *Petit* means "small" in French. Today, when a short man is very bossy he is sometimes said to have a "Napoleon complex."

Napoleon's personal life moved at a relaxed pace. He was invited to many parties and dances. However, the future leader was not very interested in socializing. In fact, he was somewhat of a loner. He went back to Corsica and started writing a history of the island.

In 1785, Napoleon's father, Carlo, died. Napoleon's brother Joseph was not able to support the family, so Napoleon had to step in and assume those responsibilities. Once again, the family was poor. Napoleon struggled to make enough money to help his mother and siblings. And even though he still wasn't very interested in a social life, he now had even less time for friends or fun.

CHAPTER TWO

Class Rebellion in France

In the 1780s, the people of France were very unhappy with the way things were being handled in their country. During that time, King Louis XVI ruled France. Most people felt that he wasn't doing a very good job as their leader.

The Three Estates

The people of France were divided into three *Estates*, or social classes. The First Estate included the clergy. The Second Estate included all the wealthy nobles who held important government offices. Many people in the First and Second Estates got very rich because they did not have to pay taxes. Combined, these Estates made up about two percent of the people in France.

The other ninety-eight percent of France's citizens were part of the Third Estate. This class included the peasants, the city workers, and the middle class. The middle class was also called the *bourgeoisie* (boor•zhwah•**zee**). While two percent of the population got richer and richer, the people in the Third Estate just kept getting poorer and poorer.

The Rule of Louis XVI

The king of France, Louis XVI, was not a very popular ruler. He was thought of as weak and not very smart. He and the other nobles were always spending the country's money on fancy clothes and expensive parties.

The peasants were upset that they had no money while the clergy and nobles had so much. The bourgeoisie was upset that they were paying so much money in taxes but didn't have any power in running the country. Meanwhile, France as a country was running out of money. King Louis XVI could have forced the wealthy people to start paying taxes like everyone else, but he was too weak to do that. He began giving important government jobs to nobles who could give some of their money to the country.

King Louis XVI

However, it wasn't enough. Louis XVI took out loans on behalf of France, but the interest on those loans cost too much. The country was almost bankrupt.

Then Louis XVI made a very bad mistake. To try to raise more money for the country, he decided to call a meeting of the Estates General.

The Estates General

The Estates General was a *parliament*, or group of people who make laws. It was made up of people from each of the three Estates. They had not met as a group in 175 years. Louis XVI called a meeting of The Estates General in 1789, in Paris. Here, the groups stated their views. The nobles and the clergy wanted each Estate to have one vote, as a group. This would mean that the First and Second Estates would always win, two votes to one, over the Third Estate. But it's not surprising that the members of the Third Estate did not like this idea. Since they represented ninety-eight percent of the population, they wanted every representative at the meeting to have one vote. They had more representatives;

Did You Know?

Marie Antoinette, the wife of King Louis XVI, also liked to spend money. She did not understand what it was like to be poor. For this reason, the people of the Third Estate started to dislike her. One legend shows how little Marie Antoinette understood about the poor people of France. When she was told that the peasants did not have any bread to eat, she supposedly said, "Well, let them eat cake." No one knows if she really said this, but if she did, it shows that she had no idea what many of the people of France were going through.

this meant the Third Estate would always have more votes than the First and Second Estates. Of course, the nobles and clergy refused to agree to their plan. After a bitter argument, the entire Third Estate left the meeting in anger. They held their own meeting to decide what to do.

The "common" citizens of France had been informed about what was going on in nearby England. Though England had a king like France did, there were strict limits put on the king's power. The English citizens had more rights than the citizens of France, and they had a personal interest in what was happening with their country. The Third Estate knew that it was time for their government to represent all French people, not just the wealthy.

The National Assembly and the French Revolution

The members of the Third Estate formed a group called the *National Assembly*. They told the nobles and the clergy that they represented the entire country of France. The common people demanded equal rights and freedom from the king's rule. Louis XVI became nervous and tried to shut down the movement. He sent soldiers to try to stop the National Assembly from gathering in Paris.

It was too late. The National Assembly had armed itself with weapons to protect citizens from the soldiers. They stormed into Paris on July 14, 1789, and attacked the Bastille (ba•**steel**). This was a huge prison, where many political prisoners were being held. Many soldiers

The attack on the Bastille

were killed, and the prisoners were set free. This was the beginning of the French Revolution. July 14th is still celebrated in France as Independence Day. It is similar to July 4th in the United States.

The National Assembly soon issued a document. It was called

Did You Know?

The Bastille was a huge *fortress,* or military fort in Paris. It was built in 1370 to help make the city stronger against attacks. By the 17th century, it was being used as a prison. Before it was attacked, the Bastille was rumored to house thousands of political prisoners.

the *Declaration of Rights of Man and of Citizens*. The document stated that all people in France had the right to liberty. Liberty, it said, was the freedom to do anything that did not injure others. The document established a *legislature,* or governing body. It gave voting rights to anyone who owned property. The power of the king was also limited, and the clergy was put under government control.

By 1791, an official constitution had been written. Louis XVI made everyone think that he was going along with it. Secretly, however, he was trying to raise money to create an army of his own. He **yearned** to have all of his power back. He also wanted the National Assembly to **disband**. On June 20, 1791, he and his wife, Marie Antoinette, tried to escape from France. They were going to meet with his supporters outside of France and form a new army. But they were captured near the France-Belgium border and brought back to Paris. In September, Louis XVI was forced to sign the constitution. The people of France now saw him as a traitor, someone who had betrayed his country. Understandably, they turned against him.

> *"Men who have changed the world never achieved their success by winning the chief citizens to their side, but always by stirring the masses."*
> *–Napoleon*

CHAPTER THREE

Napoleon Begins His Military Career

When the French Revolution started, Napoleon was back in France. He was training at the artillery school in Auxonne (ohks•**un**). Napoleon was still a part of the French middle class. He agreed with what the National Assembly wanted to do. He also thought that the Revolution could be a way for Corsica to finally gain freedom from France. Napoleon wanted to be one of the leaders in Corsica, so he resigned from the French artillery. Soon he became a lieutenant colonel in the Corsican National Guard. But the leader of the Corsican Revolution, Pasquale Paoli, didn't trust Napoleon. He thought Napoleon had become "too French" during his time in France. He didn't think that he could now be completely loyal to Corsica.

Meanwhile, other European countries were beginning to attack France. A war between France and England began in 1793. The entire Buonaparte family accused Paoli of siding with England. A civil war broke out on Corsica. Paoli

A Fact For You

Doctor Joseph Ignace Guillotin (1738-1814) is credited with designing the guillotine. At the time, executions were part of the law in France. Dr. Guillotin was against these executions. He was not able to change French law. Therefore, he tried to devise a more humane way to perform them.

When victims were executed using the guillotine, they were placed on a bench, face down. Then, their necks were positioned between two pieces of wood.

The actual beheading was very quick. It took less than half a second from the blade dropping to the victim's head rolling into the waiting basket.

The invention didn't do what Dr. Guillotin had hoped. Instead, it helped to bring terror to the French Revolution. More than 13,000 people were executed using the guillotine. Dr. Guillotin's family begged the French government to change the name of the device. When they didn't, the Guillotin family changed their name.

guillotine, ca 1800s

won, and the Buonapartes were forced to escape from Corsica to France.

Napoleon cut all of his ties to Corsica and settled in France. Many of the wealthy French military leaders were fleeing the country because of the Revolution. Important military positions were now opening up for young, **ambitious** officers like Napoleon. Therefore, Napoleon's military career and rise to power began. King Louis XVI was also arrested for being a traitor.

He was executed at the **guillotine** (gee•yuh•teen) on January 21, 1793, in front of a cheering crowd.

The First Coalition

When Napoleon rejoined the French army, France was at war against a *coalition,* or group, of countries. The First Coalition was made of Austria, Prussia, Holland, Spain, Sardinia, and England. The British army had captured the city of Toulon (too•**lohn**) in southern France. The city was an important port on the coast of the Mediterranean Sea. The army that controlled Toulon had control of that part of the Mediterranean Sea.

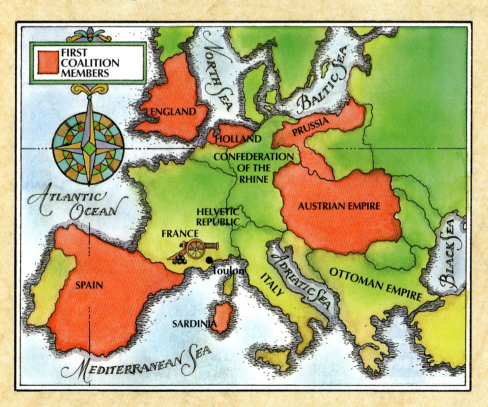

Napoleon, now 24 years old, was sent to Toulon under the command of the French General Carteaux (kar•**toh**). Napoleon had a plan for recapturing the city from the British. He thought that the French should attack the large fort that overlooked the city. It was used to resupply all the British ships. If the fort could be brought down, the British army wouldn't be able to get supplies. They would be forced to leave. Napoleon wanted the French soldiers to fire all their weapons on the fort in order to bring it down.

However, General Carteaux did not want to listen to Napoleon's plan. He thought Napoleon was too young and inexperienced to know what he was talking about. Carteaux also believed that the fort at Toulon was much too strong to be brought down by simply using gunfire. For three months, Napoleon and the rest of the army tried to capture Toulon by doing things the way Carteaux wanted. Yet, the British soldiers were constantly holding them back.

Finally, General Dugommier (doo•goh•mee•**ay**) replaced General Carteaux. Dugommier immediately realized that Napoleon's plan could work. He allowed Napoleon to carry out the plan and lead the battle. Napoleon found a sheltered place where the French army could **bombard** the fort with all their weapons.

After just a few days of firing upon the fort, a large hole had been blasted through the wall. The French soldiers poured through the hole and captured the fort from the British. Then they started firing at all the British ships in the harbor. The British soldiers quickly left Toulon on their remaining vessels.

Robespierre and the Reign of Terror

Maximilien Robespierre

Toulon surrendered to Napoleon and the French. Napoleon was given credit for the victory. His generals wrote to the French Minister of War praising Napoleon. The news of Napoleon's victory reached a man named Maximilien Robespierre (mahks•ee•mee•**lyuhn** rohbz•**pyair**). Robespierre was the military leader of France at the time. Within just a few months, Robespierre promoted Napoleon from captain all the way up to brigadier general.

However, Robespierre was quickly losing popularity in France. He had begun a period of rule that was called the *Reign of Terror*. Robespierre believed strongly in the death penalty. He thought that anyone who opposed him should be taken to the guillotine immediately. Many other crimes, such as stealing, were also punishable by execution. Anyone who was in favor of a sovereign king, someone who could rule without any limits, was also executed immediately, without a trial.

"There is no strength without justice."
–Napoleon

Many of the high-ranking officials in Paris began turning on Robespierre. They wanted his horrible Reign of Terror to end. On July 28, 1794, Robespierre was arrested and taken to the guillotine. Followers of Robespierre, called *Robespierrists,* were thrown into prison. Since Napoleon was a high-ranking officer under Robespierre, he also went to prison. Luckily, his ties to Robespierre were not that strong. While in prison, Napoleon wrote an angry letter to the new military leaders. After just ten days in prison, Napoleon was set free. Although he had been released, he was still considered somewhat of a Robespierrist. He was forced to take a low-ranking job making less money.

National Convention

Napoleon was working for the Committee of Public Safety in Paris when a riot broke out in late 1795. The new government that had risen to power after Robespierre's death was called the *National Convention.* Like the National Assembly before it, it gave most of the power to the middle class. The peasants were tired of being promised more food and more money when what they were really getting was a food shortage and higher prices. Huge mobs of peasants marched to the National Convention. They were hoping to take some control away from the middle class. Napoleon heard about the rioting and went to the National Convention. Government troops were trying to hold back the rioters, but their leader had left. They needed a new leader. A man named Paul Barras knew of Napoleon's victory at Toulon. He saw Napoleon in the crowd and asked him to defend the Convention against the rioters.

The next day, about 25,000 angry peasants marched to the Convention building from two different directions.

Napoleon only had 5,000 soldiers under his command. But he had wisely anticipated the routes the mob would take. He ordered the mob to retreat. When they didn't follow his orders, Napoleon ordered his soldiers to fire at the mob.

Nearly 1,000 French peasants were either killed or wounded by the gunfire. The rest ran away from the Convention in a panic. Napoleon's actions had meant the deaths of many French citizens. Yet, he was still considered a hero. The Convention had been saved. The middle class was able to get their new constitution passed. Napoleon was promoted to commander of the Army of the Interior. He was in charge of all French soldiers stationed within the country of France.

Around the same time Napoleon was busy saving the Convention, he was also busy doing something else: falling in love.

Josephine

Josephine de Beauharnais was beautiful and charming. She had been married to a general who was one of the early leaders of the French Revolution. Like many early Revolution leaders, he had been executed at the guillotine. Josephine was widowed and left with two children, a son named Eugene and a daughter named Hortense.

Josephine de Beauharnais

When Napoleon and Josephine first met in Paris, each thought the other was rich. Josephine had once been wealthy, but she had lost everything after her husband was killed. She thought that Napoleon could make her wealthy again. Because Napoleon knew how important Josephine's husband had once been, he thought Josephine was rich. He was still responsible for supporting his mother and siblings, and he thought that she was the answer to his problems. He also thought she could help him enter the high society of Paris. This would give him

IF IT WEREN'T FOR NAPOLEON...

Napoleon's armies were often hungry. Their food spoiled very quickly in the hot sun. Napoleon knew that he needed to keep his armies healthy and well fed. Around the year 1795, Napoleon offered a reward to anyone who could come up with a successful way to preserve food.

A French chef named Nicholas Appert (ah•pair) was the winner of the 12,000 francs. (This would equal about $1,700 today.) His invention was the basis for the process of canning that we still use today.

Appert knew that wine could be preserved for a long time in glass bottles topped with corks. He devised a way for meats and vegetables to be preserved in much the same way.

Napoleon tried to keep Appert's invention a military secret. However, the news eventually got out and made it across the English Channel. In 1804, Appert opened a vacuum-packing plant in France. Others improved on his invention and began using tin cans instead. It was reported that both sides at the Battle of Waterloo relied on canned rations.

the opportunity to meet wealthy people who would help advance his military career.

By the time Napoleon and Josephine found out that neither was rich, it was too late. They had fallen in love with one another. They were married on March 9, 1796. She was 33 and he was 27. Ironically, on their marriage license, they both lied. She wrote that she was 29, and he wrote that he was 28.

Even though he was now married, Napoleon still felt something was missing from his life. He didn't think that being the commander of the French soldiers was very exciting. Napoleon recognized the importance of conquering other lands for France. The more territory France controlled, the more resources his country controlled, and the wealthier France became. Napoleon also knew a military leader was only as important as the lands he conquered, so he longed for the recognition.

France had declared war on Austria four years earlier to achieve control over the country of Italy. At the time, Austria had control. France had sent more than 100,000 soldiers to Italy. The previous French military leader was relieved of his duties, so a new leader was needed. Napoleon willingly accepted the assignment. Just two days after his marriage to Josephine, Napoleon left for Italy.

CHAPTER FOUR

Napoleon Comes Into Power

Napoleon standing on the bridge at Arcola

When Napoleon arrived in Italy, **morale** among the French soldiers was very low. Of more than 100,000 original soldiers, fewer than half remained. Some had died in battle. Some had died from disease. Still others had *deserted,* or abandoned, the army and had gone home. The soldiers had not been paid for months. They were almost out of supplies and equipment. Their previous commander had divided the men into small groups to spread them over the border between Italy and France. However, the smaller groups of soldiers were much more *vulnerable,* or open, to attacks by the Austrians and the British.

Napoleon Wins Over the Troops

The French army officers in Italy did not know what to expect from Napoleon. When he arrived to take charge, they realized he was much younger than they were. He also didn't have as much experience as they did. Some of them thought they deserved to be put in command of the troops in Italy. However, there were things about Napoleon that made the men trust him. He was very confident and seemed to know what he was doing. In a smart move, he raised the soldiers' morale right away by arranging for them to be paid some of the wages they were owed. He also promised them that if the French army could take over Italy, the soldiers could keep some of Italy's riches and treasures for themselves. It was a promise that he would keep.

"Soldiers generally win battles; generals get credit for them."
–Napoleon

Facing the Austrian Army

The Austrian army was twice as big as the French army. It included soldiers from Sardinia, an island west of Italy. However, the Austrian-Sardinian army was overconfident about their size. They thought they could afford to be spread out into three smaller parts. Napoleon saw the flaw in their thinking. The French army could never defeat the entire Austrian-Sardinian army at once. However, he realized that his entire French army might be able to defeat the smaller, divided armies. Within just two weeks, the French army had forced the Sardinian part of the Austrian army to retreat.

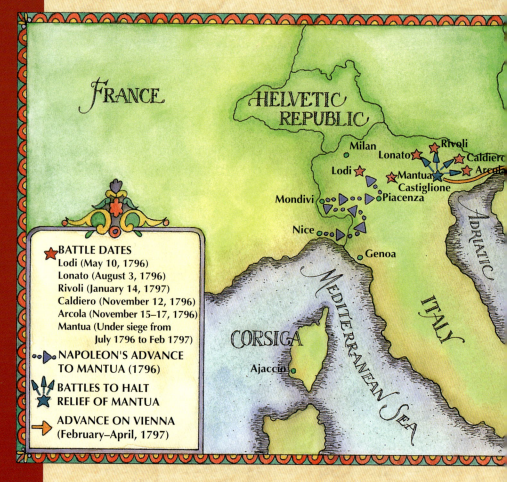

BATTLE DATES
Lodi (May 10, 1796)
Lonato (August 3, 1796)
Rivoli (January 14, 1797)
Caldiero (November 12, 1796)
Arcola (November 15–17, 1796)
Mantua (Under siege from July 1796 to Feb 1797)

NAPOLEON'S ADVANCE TO MANTUA (1796)

BATTLES TO HALT RELIEF OF MANTUA

ADVANCE ON VIENNA (February–April, 1797)

A short time later, Napoleon and his men confronted the largest part of the Austrian army at a place called Lodi (**loh**•dee). The Austrians were on the far side of a river. The Austrian army thought that the only way for the French to get to them was over a narrow bridge. The Austrians knew that if the French army crossed the bridge, they could be fired at easily. But Napoleon had a surprise for them. He led his men along the river until

they found a safe place to cross. His army attacked the Austrians unexpectedly from the side. The French defeated the Austrians there, and Napoleon's men were pleased. They had begun to win battles against Austria. Napoleon was not afraid to fight right alongside his soldiers, and they respected him greatly. In fact, he was in the very front of the troops when the battle started.

In August, a new and larger Austrian army was brought in to challenge the French army. The Austrians had learned their lesson. The army was three times bigger than Napoleon's. A man named Count Dagobart Sigismund von Wurmser (**dah**•goh•bart **zee**•gis•moont fon **voorm**•zuhr) led them. He had won many battles against the French before. But once again, Napoleon had a surprise for the Austrians. The French army attacked the city of Castiglione (kah•stee•**lyoh**•nay). They won, and 15,000 Austrians were taken as prisoners. Napoleon quickly attacked von Wurmser and his men two more times. Von Wurmser finally retreated to a city named Mantua (**mahn**•too•ah). Napoleon and his men followed the Austrian army there and held them under siege (seej). This means that the French surrounded the Austrians so that they were trapped. Another Austrian army of 60,000 men appeared a short time later. Napoleon's army fought in a three-day battle with them at a place called Arcola (ar•**koh**•luh), then at Rivoli (**ree**•voh•lee). The Austrians lost 30,000 soldiers. The rest were forced to return to Austria. Von Wurmser and his men were still trapped in Mantua. He had no choice but to surrender to Napoleon. France had defeated Austria. Now, all of northern Italy was under Napoleon's control.

Napoleon explained to the people of Italy that he was there to free them from the Austrians. However, freedom had a price. Everyone in Italy was forced to pay taxes to France. The richest people in northern Italy were taxed most severely. All of the taxes collected from the Italians were sent back to France by Napoleon.

Napoleon Keeps His Promise

Just as Napoleon promised, his men were allowed to keep most of the valuables that they found. Expensive art treasures like paintings, statues, and jewelry were boxed up and shipped to Paris. Many of the paintings still hang in the Louvre (**loo**•vr) museum in Paris today. The value of the stolen art treasures was about ten million dollars at the time. Their value today would of course be much higher than that.

In France, Napoleon was being hailed as a hero. The news of his victories in Italy had made it back there quickly. Still, things were not going well for the French government. There were still a lot of food shortages, and more people were unemployed than ever before. Some people were wondering if perhaps France had been better off with a king after all. The people wanted a strong leader who could make everything right again.

The Louvre

The Louvre is the most famous art museum in the world. But before it was an art museum, it was a palace for kings. It has been said that the halls in the Louvre are so wide that one king used them for horseraces with his children. During the reign of each king, improvements were made to its structure. When the French Revolution began, the Louvre became a museum. Many of the treasures that Napoleon and his troops took from their battles were added to the Louvre's exhibits.

Napoleon Leaves Italy for France

Napoleon returned to France on December 5, 1797. He had been away from his wife, Josephine, for more than a year and a half. He missed her very much. He longed to have a son with her, so that there would be a man to carry on Napoleon's name and work.

Off to Battle Once Again

The French military still needed Napoleon. They asked him to lead an invasion of England. But Napoleon was too smart for that. He knew that no one had successfully invaded England since the year 1066. The British navy was the most powerful in the world. Napoleon thought he might have a better idea. Instead of invading England, he decided to invade Egypt. If France could control Egypt, they could hurt England in a different way. They could get in the way of England's trade routes to the Middle East. It would also put France in a position to conquer England's most valuable possession, the country of India.

Napoleon knew that two famous world conquerors had captured Egypt in the past. Their names were Alexander the Great and Augustus Caesar. Napoleon wanted his name to go down in history like theirs. Josephine didn't want to be without her husband again. She asked if she could go to Egypt, too. Napoleon said no. However, he did agree to take her son, Eugene, along.

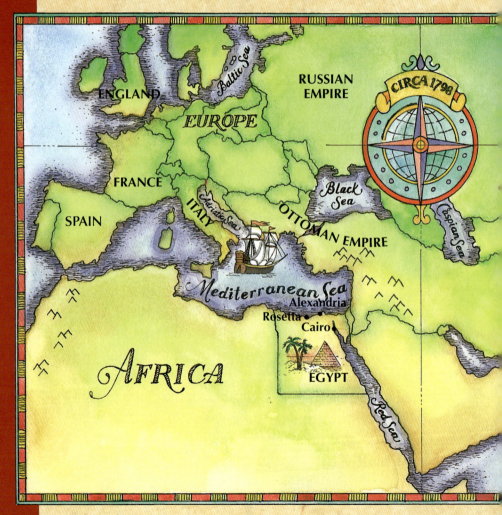

On May 19, 1798, Napoleon set sail from Toulon with his *armada* (ar•**mah**•duh), or fleet of ships. There were 130 transport ships, 85 small warships, and 7 frigates (**fri**•guhts). A *frigate* is a medium-sized warship that can sail very fast. He had nearly 40,000 soldiers. Many of them had fought with Napoleon in Italy. He also brought along historians and scientists. Napoleon was fascinated by Egypt. He was determined to learn as much as possible about its history while he was there. So, he brought 16,000 people with him to study Egypt on behalf of France.

Things went well for Napoleon when the French arrived in Egypt. He and his men conquered the country without much trouble. The scientists and historians got to work studying the country. One important discovery they made was the Rosetta Stone. While they were there, they also gathered enough information to write a 24-book account of the history of Egypt.

> "Different subjects and different affairs are arranged in my head as in a cupboard. When I wish to interrupt one train of thought, I shut that drawer and open another. Do I wish to sleep, I simply close all the drawers and then I am asleep."
> –Napoleon

The Key To A Mystery—The Rosetta Stone

One of the scholars who went with Napoleon to Egypt in 1798 found a round, flat stone near a small village named Rosetta. His name was Bouchard. The stone had *inscriptions,* or engraved writing, in three different languages: Greek, Demotic Egyptian, and hieroglyphics. *Demotic Egyptian* is a simple form of the Egyptian language. *Hieroglyphics* is an ancient type of Egyptian writing that uses pictures and symbols instead of letters.

Scientists and historians had tried for centuries to read hieroglyphics. But the language had died with the ancient Egyptians. The scientists thought the stone was interesting, but they really weren't sure what it meant. Then, Bouchard and the other scholars made the exciting observation that the same message had been written on the stone in the three different languages. Because the scholars could read Greek, they realized they now had the key to reading hieroglyphics.

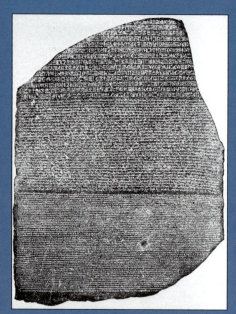

Rosetta Stone

They were able to use what they learned about hieroglyphics to read other texts that were written in the picture language.

The discovery of the Rosetta Stone unlocked the mysteries of Egyptian hieroglyphics. Today, when someone finds the key to a mystery or the solution to a complex problem, they might refer to it as "finding their Rosetta Stone."

Back in France, Napoleon was again being called a hero. The French didn't know that they were only hearing about the victories in Egypt. Napoleon and his men had started out well. But now they were in big trouble. In July, a British admiral named Horatio Nelson and his navy surrounded the French fleet of ships at Alexandria, Egypt. During a big battle, called the *Battle of the Nile*, all but two of the French ships were destroyed. The French admiral was killed, along with nearly 2,000 of his men. The British only lost 218 of their men. It was a devastating defeat.

Battle of Cairo, 1798

Napoleon's troops were completely cut off from all their supplies. They were trapped, with no way to escape. The people of Egypt did not make it easy for them either. They were very hostile toward the French troops that had invaded their country. Napoleon tried to march east with 13,000 of his men, but they kept being forced back. They finally returned to Cairo.

Trouble in Italy Once Again

Meanwhile, all the work that Napoleon had done in Italy was being undone. The British had taken over the country, and they had driven the French out of Italy. Napoleon knew he had lost the war against the British in Egypt. He promised his men that he would return to rescue them if he could. Then he set sail for France in one of his two remaining ships.

When Napoleon arrived home, he was treated as an even bigger hero than before. The public still did not know that Napoleon's men were trapped in Egypt. This time Napoleon didn't live up to his promise. He never returned to Egypt. Napoleon's men remained trapped until they surrendered to the British two years after he left them. But Napoleon had more important things to do. He was the hero of France, and he was about to become its leader.

Fact or Fiction?

Did Napoleon and his men damage the Sphinx when they were in Egypt? The Great Sphinx is a very large sculpture carved from rock. It stands near the pyramids in Egypt. The sculpture was probably built around 2500 B.C. It has the head of a man and the body of a lion. Unfortunately, at some point in history, the Sphinx lost its nose. According to one popular legend, Napoleon's men shot the nose off the Sphinx while using the sculpture for target practice.

No one is sure how or when the Sphinx lost its nose. However, most historians agree that it was gone before Napoleon arrived to conquer Egypt in 1798. Many writings from the 14th and 15th centuries describe the Sphinx's face as having been vandalized. In addition, the artist named Frederick Norden painted the Sphinx after visiting Egypt in 1737. This was 60 years before Napoleon visited. Even in Norden's painting, the sculpture didn't have a nose.

CHAPTER FIVE
Napoleon as First Consul

It didn't take long for Napoleon to start thinking about becoming the leader of France. The politicians in France were fighting among themselves. Some wanted France to return to a monarchy system and have a king. Others wanted to continue the way things were going, with a government made up of many different elected officials working together.

A man named Emmanuel Sieyès (sye•**yes**) was a politician who had once been a priest. Sieyès thought the political fighting could be solved if fewer people ran the government. He wanted to replace the five current leaders, called the *Directory*, with a Consulate of three men, called *consuls*. But his idea went even further than that. Under the current government, the Directory was responsible for making up the laws. However, the legislature, made up of the Council of Ancients and the Council of Five Hundred, was responsible for passing the laws. Sieyès wanted the legislature **abolished,** or done away with. Napoleon supported Sieyès because he thought he had a good chance of becoming one of the three consuls. He and Sieyès also believed that with only three consuls, one man would eventually become the leader.

Napoleon gave a speech to the Council of Five Hundred. He tried to persuade them to accept the Consulate. But they drove him out of the hall. Napoleon's younger brother Lucien (loo•**syen**) was president of the Council of Five Hundred. He gave a speech to the Council on behalf of his brother. He then marched outside, where Napoleon's loyal soldiers were waiting. Lucien told them that the Council was standing in the way of freedom for all citizens of France. The soldiers marched into the hall and forced the members of the Council to leave the building. Some of the members were allowed back in. Only those who agreed to vote for the Consulate idea were permitted to return. A vote was taken, and it was decided that the Directory and the Councils of Five Hundred and Ancients would step down, and the Consulate would take charge of the government.

Napoleon was named the First Consul. Sieyès was named the Second Consul. A man named Roger Ducos (roh•**zhay** doo•**koh**) was named the Third Consul. Sieyès wrote a new constitution, and Napoleon made a few changes and corrections. The three Consuls quickly put the new constitution into effect. Two months later, in February 1800, the people of France voted on the new constitution. The **polls** stayed open for a month. However, only half of all eligible voters went to the polls to place their vote. In the end, it was 3,500,000 votes in favor of the new constitution and only 1,500 votes against it.

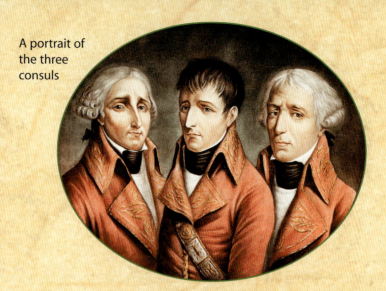

A portrait of the three consuls

Many changes had been made to create the new constitution. The country was divided into smaller sections. The election process changed as well. Although every adult male was now allowed to vote, the election system was flawed with complications and issues of fairness.

Napoleon, as First Consul, could choose 40 members to be part of the Council of State. The Council of State would be responsible for submitting *bills*, or laws, to the legislature. The legislature was divided into three parts. The Senate was chosen by the Second and Third Consuls from a list of elected men. They decided if the laws submitted by the Council of State were constitutional. The Tribunate was chosen by the Senate. They could discuss any proposed new laws, but they could not vote on them. The Legislative Body was also chosen by the Senate. They could vote on the proposed new laws, but they could not discuss them.

"The word impossible is not in my dictionary."
—Napoleon

First Consul for Life

Napoleon was also appointed Minister of the Interior. In the United States, the government officials and mayors are voted into office. But under the consul form of government in France, the Minister of Interior chose these positions. It looked like a fair system, because it seemed as though the responsibilities for running the country were falling on many different people. But in reality, Napoleon was in charge of everyone. He was, for all practical purposes, the **dictator** of France. Napoleon now had all the power.

The position of First Consul was supposed to last for ten years. But in 1802, a vote was held. Napoleon was named First Consul for Life. There are many reasons why Napoleon was popular with the French. He lowered income taxes. This made Napoleon very well liked among those who didn't make much money. Many people who had supported the Revolution were forced to leave France when the

Revolution ended. Napoleon let them all come back home. He also canceled a yearly festival that celebrated the execution of King Louis XVI. He established a system of national education that included elementary schools, high schools, colleges, and technical schools. He established better training for teachers. He passed several laws that helped businessmen become more successful. He also established the Bank of France.

One of Napoleon's greatest achievements was called the *Code Napoleon*. Laws in France at the time varied greatly from one place to another. For instance, an act that was legal in one city in France could be illegal and punishable by prison in another. So, Napoleon appointed a group named the *Commission of Legislation*. He wanted them to study all the existing laws and make them the same throughout the country. It took until the year 1810 to complete the Code Napoleon, and it is still the basis of many French laws today. The Code Napoleon is also the basis of law in Belgium, the Netherlands, Italy, and many South American countries.

By 1799, when Napoleon became First Consul of France, the country had been at war for almost ten years. France had fought against nearly every country in Europe. But England continued to be its most **persistent** and dangerous enemy. England was a strong country with a good economy. The English leaders saw France as their biggest threat. No other country in Europe was big enough or strong enough to overpower the British.

In 1800, Napoleon took his soldiers across the Alps

to Austria. It was a difficult trip. His troops faced snow, ice avalanches, and winds. Finally, they arrived in Marengo (muh•**reng**•goh), exhausted, hungry, and frozen. A battle against the Austrians was fought there. At the last minute, Napoleon's troops were victorious. The French also fought them at a place called Hohenlinden (**hoh**•uhn•lin•duhn). Like so many times before, the French defeated the Austrians. Austria called for peace. In March 1802, a *peace treaty*, or agreement, was signed. It was called the *Treaty of Amiens* (ah•**myan**). The terms of the treaty stated England was to give up most of their conquests made in the wars, and France would restore Egypt to the Ottoman Empire. For a while, all of the wars in Europe ended.

Napoleon and his troops crossed the Alps. Notice his hat in this picture. Napoleon wore a type of hat called a *tricorne*. Several years ago, his hat was sold at an auction for $29,471, becoming the most expensive hat ever sold.

But peace only lasted for about fifteen months. Austria had been an **ally** of England. After Austria's defeat, England's power over Europe was not as strong as it had once been.

The Louisiana Purchase

During the time of peace, Napoleon was busy in Paris. In 1803, he did some business with the United States. It was called the *Louisiana Purchase*. For fifteen million dollars, Napoleon sold all the land controlled by France between the Mississippi River and the Rocky Mountains. The sale doubled the size of the then United States.

Many people thought Napoleon had made a huge mistake. Even back in 1803, the price seemed low for so much territory. The sale also took away any chance France ever had of being in control of the land on the other side of the Atlantic Ocean. However, from Napoleon's point of view, the sale was a good move for France. First of all, France didn't really "own" the land. They had claimed it, but it would have been very hard for France to hold on to it. The British navy was in control of the oceans between Europe and the United States. Napoleon knew that his military would never be able to cross the ocean to protect the land.

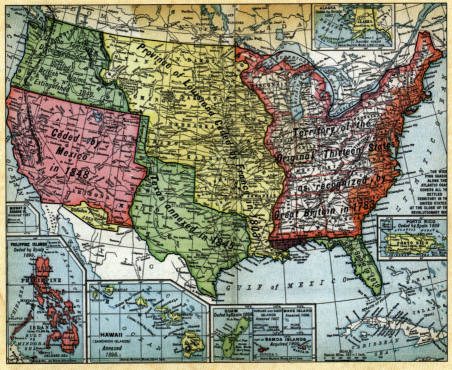

Map of the United States expansion

Napoleon also knew that the United States was growing. He thought it was very possible that the United States might try to take the territory from France anyway. It was also possible that England might try to take the land. If England gained control of the land, their power would grow even stronger. If the United States took control of the land by force, France would receive no money for the land. In selling the land, Napoleon had given up something he didn't really own anyway. He had also put fifteen million dollars into France's economy.

The End of Peace

Napoleon knew that the peace in Europe would not last very long. Someday soon, France would have to meet England in battle again. Napoleon began preparing for the battles that he knew would come. He started a large program to build new ships for France. Many of them were large flat-bottomed boats called *barges*. These boats could carry large numbers of soldiers across the English Channel to England, if it were ever necessary.

Napoleon also worried about what would happen to France after his death. He wanted to make sure that his future children would automatically follow him as leader of the country. The only way to ensure this was for Napoleon to become the emperor of France.

DID YOU KNOW?

Napoleon loved to take baths. One day in 1803, Napoleon was sitting in the tub. His brothers Joseph and Lucien barged in, all in a rage. They were upset because Napoleon planned to sell Louisiana to the Americans. Legend has it that Napoleon splashed his bath water all over Joseph.

CHAPTER SIX

Napoleon, Emperor of France

Napoleon's popularity was decreasing among the French population. He realized this and decided that if he was to become emperor, he had to take matters into his own hands. Therefore, he proclaimed himself emperor of the French. Napoleon was crowned emperor of France on December 2, 1804. He was only 35 years old. When he arrived at Notre Dame Cathedral in Paris for the ceremony, he was riding in a carriage decorated with a large purple "N."

More than 8,000 people were present in the cathedral for the coronation. Napoleon sat on a golden throne. He was wearing a robe. Josephine, soon to be empress, sat five steps below her husband, on a smaller throne.

Pope Pius VII presided over the ceremony. Just as everyone in the cathedral thought the Pope was about to place the crown on Napoleon's head, something unusual happened. Napoleon picked up the crown from the tray it was on and placed it on his own head!

Napoleon crowning Josephine empress

He had crowned himself emperor! It was Napoleon's way of showing everyone that no one, not even the pope, had power over Napoleon. Napoleon then crowned Josephine empress by placing a diamond crown on her head. The pope kissed the new emperor's cheek and said, "Long live the emperor."

The British were very worried when Napoleon became emperor. They didn't want him to gain any more power in Europe. So they formed a new *coalition*, or group of allies, against France. Like before, England was joined by Austria. This time, they were also joined by Russia. Prussia, one of the strongest German states, joined as well.

Napoleon wanted to stop this coalition before it even started. This time, he thought he might have enough power to stop England for good. He decided to invade the country. Napoleon felt that his army was stronger than England's, but he was concerned about getting his men across the English Channel and onto British soil.

The Battle of Trafalgar

The French naval fleet was commanded by a man named Pierre de Villeneuve (**pyair** duh veel•uh•**nuv**). Once again, Admiral Horatio Nelson led the British. The British navy pursued Villeneuve and his men. They ended up in Spain, at a port named Cádiz (kuh•**diz**). Spain was an ally of France at the time, so Villeneuve was able to double his fleet by adding fourteen Spanish warships.

They met the British again near Trafalgar (truh•**fal**•guhr), a cape in southern Spain. Even though the French fleet was larger than the British fleet, Admiral Nelson's men were much better sailors and more experienced. Nelson utilized a strategy to divide his fleet into two sections and penetrated the enemy line from two directions. They **outmaneuvered** the French fleet and ended up destroying more than half of Villeneuve's ships. The British, however, did not lose even one ship during the battle!

The French Revolutionary Calendar

The leaders of the Revolution decided that France needed a new calendar system. They wanted to **eliminate** the names of days and months that had anything to do with religion or mythology.

Like the Gregorian calendar used in many parts of the world today, the Revolutionary calendar had twelve months. But each new year began on the first day of autumn—around what is our September 22.

Each month had 30 days. The months were not divided into weeks. They were divided into blocks of ten days, called *decades*. The tenth day of each decade was a day of rest. This meant that the French worked nine days before they got a day off.

It didn't take long for the people of France to get tired of the new calendar. They didn't like having to work nine days without a break. Plus, the rest of the world was still using the Gregorian calendar. It was confusing when French people tried to do business with someone outside of France.

On January 1, 1806, Napoleon abolished the Revolutionary calendar and France returned to using the Gregorian calendar.

Admiral Nelson was killed during the fighting, but he was considered a true hero to England. Today, there is a square in London named *Trafalgar Square*. A statue of Admiral Nelson was erected there in his honor. England had once again proven to Napoleon that they were in charge of the seas. Napoleon gave up all hope of ever invading England again.

Land Wars

After the Battle of Trafalgar, Napoleon came up with a new strategy. He decided that France was much better at fighting wars on land. If he could keep defeating the countries that were allies of England, he might be able to weaken England's power in Europe. He took his army and marched into Austria. Then he turned north to a small village named Austerlitz (**ows**•tuhr•lits) in what is now the Czech Republic. There, he and his men battled a large army of Austrians and Russians. This encounter was called the *Battle of Austerlitz*.

The Battle of Austerlitz is considered by many historians to be Napoleon's greatest military victory. He cleverly hid most of his soldiers behind a hill in the middle of the village. The Russians and Austrians attacked where they thought the French army was the weakest. However, the place where they attacked was actually the strongest. The hidden soldiers appeared from behind the hill. The enemies were under assault from all sides. They tried to escape across a frozen lake, but thousands of them fell through the ice and died. The Austrians and Russians lost almost 27,000 men during the battle. The French lost fewer than 9,000. Austria was knocked out of the war, and they signed another peace treaty. What was left of the Russian army returned home.

> *"Never interrupt your enemy when he is making a mistake."*
> *–Napoleon*

The way England saw it, Napoleon was in complete control of Europe. By the end of 1807, no army in Europe could stand up against France.

To spread his power even further, Napoleon began placing his own relatives in charge of other countries. His brother Louis was crowned king of the Netherlands in 1806. Brother Jerome was made king of some German states in 1807. Josephine's son, Eugene, was made **viceroy** of the kingdom of Italy.

But Napoleon was frustrated. He could not invade or control England. The British fleet was still in charge of the seas. So Napoleon decided to attack England another way—by hurting their import and export businesses. He called his new plan the *Continental System*. Any ports that France controlled in Europe were closed off to England. No goods could move into or out of those countries on behalf of England. Napoleon's economic advisers told him that if England could no longer sell their goods to other countries, they would quickly become economically desperate. This would mean they could not afford to continue fighting France. Their citizens would lose their jobs, run out of money, and be miserable.

However, England was a strong country. Even with Napoleon's Continental System, they were able to survive. There were still countries, like Portugal, that were friendly to England. Portugal imported goods from England. Then, they would send them to other countries in Europe on behalf of England. This did not make Napoleon happy.

He sent French troops to Portugal in 1807. When they arrived, the Portuguese royal family escaped from the country and went to live in Brazil.

Once Napoleon had easily conquered Portugal, he felt he could do the same to Spain, the country right next to it. He put his brother Joseph on the throne as king of Spain in 1808. The Spanish people were furious. How could Napoleon replace their king with someone who was from a foreign country and spoke French? Spanish citizens all over the country began to protest. The French army had little hope of defeating the Spanish. There was fighting going on all over the country. England saw their chance and sent 14,000 men to Portugal. From there, they traveled to Spain and helped defeat the French.

Napoleon continued to send more and more of his soldiers to Spain to fight the Spanish and the British. At one point, he had more than 250,000 of his soldiers on the *Iberian Peninsula* (eye•**beer**•ee•uhn puh•**nin**•suh•luh), which is the name given to the land shared by Spain and Portugal.

Napoleon started to get very nervous. While most of his soldiers were busy in Spain, other European countries were threatening to form another coalition and attack France.

> **DID YOU KNOW?**
> When the French invaded Spain, the Spanish crown jewels were walled up somewhere inside the royal palace. When Napoleon's armies occupied Spain, the jewels were hidden. The French redecorated and no clues to the jewel's whereabouts remained.

Things were not going well in Napoleon's personal life either. Josephine still had not been able to produce a son who would one day be able to take over as emperor.

Picture Perfect

Why did Napoleon always put his hand inside the front of his jacket when he was posing for a portrait?

Many different theories presented over the years have tried to explain this mystery:

1. He had an itchy rash on his stomach.
2. He had a deformed hand.
3. He felt that it was impolite to put your hands in your pockets.
4. He had a stomach ulcer and pushing on it helped relieve the pain.
5. He was winding his pocket watch.
6. He didn't think that portrait painters knew how to paint hands correctly.

Many historians agree, however, that the most likely reason Napoleon did this is very simple. During that period of history, men of fine breeding and good manners always stood that way, and Napoleon wanted to be thought of as being well bred and well mannered.

CHAPTER SEVEN

An End and a New Beginning

As time went on, Napoleon's empire grew. Yet, he was increasingly anxious about his lack of an **heir**. After all, he was now in his forties. If something happened to him, who would be his **successor**? He knew his brothers wouldn't make good rulers. He also knew that if he had a son, the people of France would accept the child as their next ruler. Napoleon worried that his death would destroy the empire that he had so carefully built with all of his strategy, energy, and resolve.

Napoleon decided that the future of France rested on his ability to produce an heir. Like it or not, even though he truly loved Josephine and knew she was loyal to him, his only choice was to divorce her.

The Road to Divorce

Napoleon and Josephine's marriage was not without dishonesty and unhappiness. Despite that, they still loved each other. When forced to make a decision, Napoleon was more concerned about protecting his empire than he was in preserving his marriage. And so, it was decided. Napoleon would divorce Josephine for the good of France.

It was a dramatic scene when he broke the news. On November 30, 1809, Napoleon and Josephine dined together. Napoleon told her of his decision to divorce her.

Napoleon divorced Josephine on December 15, 1809.

The palace staff reported they heard a scream coming from the couple's private quarters, after dinner. Rushing in, they found Josephine on the floor, crying. She had to be carried to her room. Napoleon also appeared to be genuinely upset.

The following day servants took Josephine's belongings to Malmaison (mal•ma•**zon**), which would be her home. She continued to make public appearances as empress, but everyone knew that her marriage to Napoleon was over.

On December 15, 1809, Napoleon formally announced his intention to divorce Empress Josephine. The next day, the Senate granted their divorce. The divorce ceremony was a grand but **solemn** occasion. Each of them read a statement of devotion dedicated to the other. Both of them shed many tears.

Throughout her life, Josephine surrounded herself with her favorite flower: violets. Napoleon visited Malmaison and collected violets from Josephine's garden. He would wear them in a locket until his death to remind him of their enduring love.

Marie Louise

Napoleon's choice of a second wife was well planned and brilliant. This time, he was determined to marry into one of the ruling families of Europe. Napoleon set his sights on the fifteen-year-old sister of the Russian czar. The Russian family met his proposal with excuses and delays. So, he turned his eyes to Archduchess Marie Louise of Austria, daughter of his old enemy, Emperor Francis I of Austria.

The marriage would be important for a number of reasons. It would align France with one of the oldest ruling families in Europe. It would also increase Napoleon's power. This time, Napoleon was not going to be rejected. He sent a representative to the Austrian Embassy to demand Marie Louise's hand in marriage. He didn't even wait for a reply before having a marriage contract drawn up. Word was sent that the Austrian ambassador had accepted the offer. Napoleon was overjoyed.

Archduchess Marie Louise

Marie Louise wasn't beautiful, but she was healthy. Most of her life, she had been taught that Napoleon Bonaparte was a terrible, evil man. However, she was smart. She knew how important her position could be in the power struggles between the countries of Europe. She agreed to marry Napoleon because a connection to France would be very valuable to Austria.

In the spring of 1810, Marie Louise was married to Napoleon by proxy. This means that Napoleon wasn't even at the wedding! He was represented by one of his officers. Two weeks later, a parade of 83 carriages made its way to Paris. Napoleon met Marie Louise at Compiégne (kawn•**pyen**•yuh).

The marriage of Napoleon to Marie Louise

When Napoleon arrived, the couple was married again—twice. They had one legal ceremony and one religious ceremony. The religious ceremony posed some problems. Many of the important leaders of the church in Paris refused to attend. They did not approve of the marriage because the pope had not agreed to Napoleon's divorce from Josephine. Napoleon was furious. He had them banished to the far provinces of France.

Despite the unusual circumstances of their marriage, the couple seemed happy. After their wedding, Marie Louise wrote her father. She wrote that Napoleon loved her very much and that she felt the same way. Napoleon had managed to charm his new bride as completely as he charmed so many others. When the stakes were high and he had much to gain, Napoleon was at his best.

Impressed by the fact that she was a real princess, Napoleon went out of his way to treat Marie Louise royally. He took great pains to please her. Hoping to begin things on a positive note, he arranged for the entire staff to meet her needs.

Napoleon had his researchers discover what gifts Louis XVI had given to welcome Marie Antoinette. He then made sure that Marie Louise got the same. He had her personal rooms redecorated and lavished her with costly gifts. He also tried to make himself more attractive. Determined to make himself more elegant, he arranged for a new tailor and a new shoemaker. He even learned the latest dance—the waltz.

59

Marie Louise was never as popular with the French as Josephine had been. But she was not a bad empress. Eventually, the people came to regard her as a symbol of France's triumph over foreign foes.

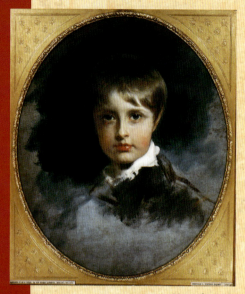

Napoleon II

Birth of an Heir

On March 20, 1811, Marie Louise's popularity in France soared. On that day, she gave birth to Francois Charles Joseph, also known as Napoleon II. The baby was immediately proclaimed the king of Rome.

Napoleon was delighted in his son and his young wife. But Marie Louise was jealous of Napoleon's frequent visits with Josephine. Napoleon even arranged for Josephine to meet the young prince. Napoleon eventually limited his trips. However, he continued to write letters to Josephine.

The Russian Initiative

The news of Napoleon's marriage to Marie Louise did not please everyone. Czar Alexander I of Russia was one person who became quite upset over their union. He was afraid that if France united with Austria, it could pose a threat to Russia.

In fact, he was so worried that he organized an army of 240,000 men. He knew he didn't have enough men to defeat Napoleon. But he had a brilliant plan. In Napoleon's previous victories over Russia, the czar's armies had always been on the offensive. This time the czar planned to draw Napoleon's troops into the huge expanses of Russia.

Czar Alexander I was correct in his fears about Napoleon. In December of 1811, the French leader began planning his invasion of Russia. It would be the largest military venture in history up to that time.

The March to Russia

On June 24, 1812, the invasion began. Napoleon and an army of 500,000 crossed the Niemen (**nee**•muhn) River and entered Russia. If the Russians had fought Napoleon at the border, he would have defeated them effortlessly. But, instead of staying to fight, the Russian troops retreated. During their retreat they destroyed crops, equipment, and livestock. Why would the Russians destroy their own property? Napoleon and his men soon found out. They ran out of food quickly. The Russian countryside had been destroyed. There was nothing left to replenish their supplies. The French had other problems, too. Even though the Russian troops had retreated, the French were still being attacked. Armed and angry peasants, called *Cossacks* (**kos**•aks), were keeping them very busy.

"I have made all the calculations; fate will do the rest."
–Napoleon

The weather conditions in Russia made it difficult for Napoleon's troops. Getting supplies into Russia was almost impossible for the weakened French soldiers. At the same time, the Russian army continued to retreat ahead of Napoleon. They burned fields and towns as they went. This made it difficult for the French to advance.

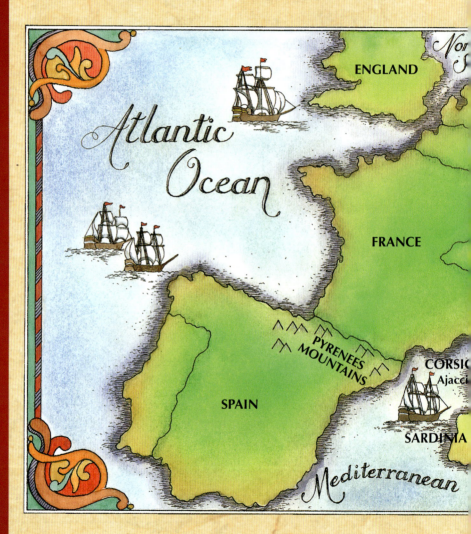

The roads began to fill with bodies and horses that were dead or dying. The Russians blocked the pathways of the French army with wagons. Despite the hardships, Napoleon's troops continued to chase their enemies deeper into Russia. After more than two months, there had not been a single battle fought.

On September 7, 1812, Napoleon finally caught up with the Russians at Borodino (buh•**ro**•dee•nuh), about 70 miles west of Moscow. The French army had now traveled some 400 miles into Russia. They had been weakened by illness, death, desertion, and ambush. Only half of Napoleon's troops remained. To add to this, Napoleon himself had several medical conditions. He was so ill that he let his generals lead the army. Eventually, the French managed to overpower the Russians. It wasn't much of a victory. The French troops lost between 30,000 and 40,000 men, and the Russians did not surrender. But Napoleon was happy about one thing—the road to Moscow was open at last.

Finally, Napoleon and his army of only 100,000 men marched through the gates of Moscow. Napoleon expected to be hailed as a conqueror. His plan was to hold the city hostage while he forced Alexander I to **negotiate** on his terms.

Instead, the city was almost deserted. The French troops moved through the deserted streets and into the empty houses. As soon as they settled in, mysterious fires began to break out everywhere. Napoleon was the unchallenged master of a city that had been reduced to little more than ashes.

To make matters worse, the czar refused to negotiate. He had his own plan. The Russian climate would defeat Napoleon's army. He would delay Napoleon in Moscow until the frigid Russian winter could finish off the hated invader. For weeks, Napoleon waited and waited for word from Alexander I, but none came. On October 18, it began to snow lightly. Napoleon knew he had no choice. The next day, he began his retreat.

He decided to try the Kaluga (kuh•**loo**•guh) Road, where there was food and water. But on October 23, at the town of Maloyaroslavets (mah•luh•yah•ro•**slah**•vetz), the Russian army forced him back to the road he had used on the way in—the shattered Smolensk (smuh•**lensk**) Road.

Napoleon and his troops approach Moscow.

By the end of October, cold weather had set in, leaving no doubt about what was to come. The temperature fell to 20 degrees below zero. Horses slipped on the ice, broke their legs, and had to be shot. Soldiers literally dropped dead from exposure and lack of food. The treasures that the troops had stolen from Moscow were discarded. The gold, silver, paintings, and jewels lay strewn everywhere. To the dying army, they held little value.

On November 26, 1812, the French army, now down to 26,000 men, reached the freezing Berezina (beh•**reh**•zee•nuh) River. Because the bridges had been destroyed, the crossing took three days. During that time, Russian troops and Cossacks kept up a constant attack. Thousands of French troops were killed, drowned, or left behind to be massacred.

Everything seemed to be going wrong for Napoleon. On one occasion, he was almost captured by Cossacks. They were always on the lookout for any French soldiers who were shorter than average. Napoleon vowed that he would never be taken prisoner. He began to wear a dose of poison around his neck in a silk pouch. He would take it if he were ever captured.

Meanwhile, news of the catastrophe in Russia had reached France and the rest of Europe. Everywhere, Napoleon's enemies rejoiced and began to plot his downfall.

"I have recognized the limits of my eyesight and of my legs, but never the limits of my working power."
–Napoleon

A group of politicians in France saw Napoleon's defeat as a way to destroy the French monarchy. A man named General Malet (mah•**lay**) announced that Napoleon had been killed on the battlefield and almost succeeded in taking over the government. When Napoleon learned of the attempted coup, or takeover, he deserted what was left of his army and rushed back to Paris.

In the spring of 1813, Napoleon did manage to win some impressive victories against the Russians and Prussians. But in June of that year, the British drove the French out of Spain. Their leader was a man named Arthur Wellesley (**welz**•lee). By October, Wellesley had reached the Pyrenees (**peer**•uh•neez), at the southwestern border of France, ready to attack.

Once again, Napoleon was in trouble. The armies of the anti-French coalition were on the move in the east. To make things even worse, Napoleon's German allies were beginning to desert him.

On October 16, 1813, Napoleon took his stand at Leipzig (**lyp**•sig), in eastern Germany. His army was greatly outnumbered by the combined forces of Austria, Russia, and Prussia. Still, the French army caused them heavy losses. It just wasn't enough. After three days of fighting, Napoleon was defeated and forced to retreat. This bloody and terrible confrontation, known as the Battle of the Nations, was the beginning of the end for Napoleon.

The French army retreats from Russia.

Throughout 1813, the coalition made several generous offers of peace. In return, they demanded that France return its borders to the way they were in 1702. Napoleon refused. He still believed in his ability to win wars. He still believed in his empire. He still believed he could rally the French people. It is likely that for Napoleon, the worst thing of all was that his legend was over. His armies were now in retreat everywhere in Europe.

CHAPTER EIGHT
Napoleon Meets His Waterloo

The end was drawing near for Napoleon as emperor of France. On December 21, 1813, the allies crossed the Rhine River and entered France. On January 1, 1814, Napoleon told the members of the Legislature that he still believed he could save France. He told them that he just needed three more months. He promised that there would finally be peace in France and in Europe. But three months later, on March 31, Napoleon discovered that the allies had reached the capital city of France. He raced to Paris to help lead the fighting against the allies, but he changed his mind and left the city. He did not want to see his beloved city of Paris destroyed by war.

Two days later, the Senate deposed Napoleon as emperor of France. This means that they forcibly removed him from office. On April 11, Napoleon finally gave up and stopped resisting the Senate. He formally *abdicated*, or gave up, the throne. He was *exiled*, or banished, to an island off the coast of Italy. The name of the island was Elba. It was a very small island, only eighty-six square miles in area. Marie Louise and Napoleon II were not allowed to go with him. The three of them shared a tearful good-bye.

Before he left for Elba, Napoleon also wrote a love letter to his first wife, Josephine. In the letter, he told her that he would always love her and would never forget her. A short time later, Josephine caught a cold. Despite a doctor's care, she grew steadily worse. She died in the arms of her son, Eugene. It was reported that Napoleon learned of her death from a French newspaper. He stayed locked in his room for two days, refusing to see anyone. She died while he was in exile, and he never saw her again.

Ruler of Elba

According to the agreement between France and the allies, Napoleon was to be the ruler of Elba. They were even willing to pay him! He was to get two million French francs per year, which today would be equal to almost $300,000 in United States currency.

Everyone thought it was the end for Napoleon. But since he had led such an exciting life and had so much power over Europe and the world, Napoleon found that he just couldn't sit around on an island all day. He began to plan a big comeback. He longed to return to France.

Meanwhile, throughout Europe, the allies began dividing up the countries that Napoleon had conquered. They regained control of what was once theirs. Back in Paris, Louis XVIII was installed as the new king of France. He was the younger brother of the previous king, Louis XVI.

Louis XVIII

At first, Louis XVIII seemed to go along with whatever the Senate wanted. But then, the citizens of France, especially those who had been loyal to Napoleon, decided that they didn't want him as their king any longer.

On March 1, 1815, Napoleon left Elba. He landed near Cannes (kahn), on the French coast, accompanied by 1,100 loyal men. The group began their dramatic march from the coast to Paris. Napoleon had carefully planned their route so that they passed through areas where he knew he had many supporters. His army grew and grew as he marched along, and they did not meet any resistance at all along the way.

General Michel Ney

Louis XVIII knew that Napoleon was a threat. He sent one of his best generals, General Michel Ney (nay), to stop Napoleon's march to Paris. Ney had fought loyally alongside Napoleon for many years. But he promised Louis XVIII that he would stop Napoleon. Ney agreed to bring him back to Paris, dead or alive. When the general reached Napoleon and his men, he couldn't go through with the king's orders. Once Ney saw his old friend Napoleon, his feelings of loyalty came back to him. He decided to join Napoleon's new army and march into Paris at his side.

Did You Know?

Elba is not a large island, but when Napoleon was sent there in 1814, the island was home to more than 110,000 people. Napoleon was named the ruler of the island, and when he arrived, he tried to improve the government there. Napoleon's family could not go to Elba with him, but he was allowed to take at least 1,000 of his men to serve as his personal assistants. He wasn't very happy. He left the island after nine months and escaped to France to **reclaim** the throne.

Back on the Throne

On March 20, 1815, Napoleon and his men finally reached Paris. Napoleon just walked right in and took over the throne. Louis XVIII was forced to flee the city. The allies around Europe realized that they would have to defeat Napoleon once more. They began getting large armies ready so that they could invade France and force Napoleon out all over again.

Waterloo

Napoleon knew that the allies would come after him. He wanted to attack the allies before they could invade France. He gathered 120,000 men and marched into the Netherlands. There, more than 200,000 English and Prussian troops were ready to meet him. Their leader was Napoleon's former enemy, Arthur Wellesley. After his last encounter with Napoleon, Wellesley went back to England a hero. In fact, they made him the Duke of Wellington. A man named General Gebhard von Blücher (**gep**•hart fon **bloo**•kuhr) commanded the Prussian troops.

Napoleon's plan was to first attack Blücher's Prussian army, then face Wellesley's army. But to Napoleon's surprise, Blücher and his men suddenly retreated. Napoleon mistakenly thought that they were giving up. He had no idea that they were actually going around to join Wellesley's army. Napoleon had made a huge error.

On June 18, 1815, Napoleon and his men attacked Wellesley's army near a small town in what is now the country of Belgium. The town was named Waterloo.

Did You Know?

Over the years of his long military career, it is said that Napoleon rode more than 150 different horses! Napoleon's favorite horse was an Arabian named Marengo. He named the horse after his victory at the Battle of Marengo.

During the Battle of Waterloo, in 1815, Marengo was captured by the British and taken back to England. After the horse's death, its skeleton was presented to the National Army Museum in England.

Just as Napoleon's army prepared to attack the British, they learned that Blücher was quickly approaching with his army. The French soldiers turned and ran, but it was too late. Blücher arrived and the French were surrounded. The Battle of Waterloo was already over, and France had lost.

Today, the Battle of Waterloo is called Napoleon's greatest defeat. It ended his comeback, which had lasted only 100 days. Back in England, Wellesley was treated as

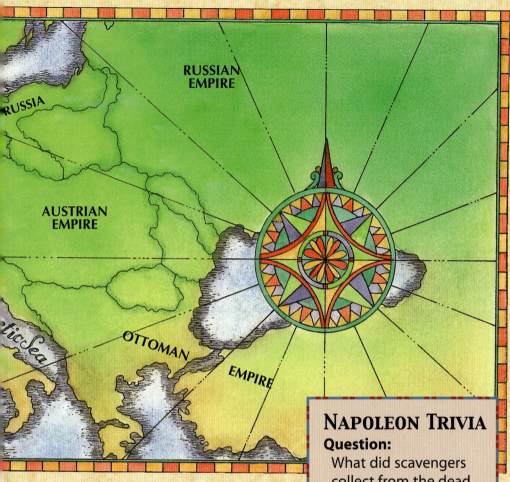

a great hero for defeating Napoleon and his men.

Napoleon survived the battle and quickly returned to Paris. There, he abdicated the throne once more. He named his son, Napoleon II, as his successor

Napoleon Trivia
Question:
What did scavengers collect from the dead after the battle of Waterloo?

Answer:
They collected teeth. For many years after the battle, false teeth were known as "Waterloo teeth."

to the throne, but it was not to be. Napoleon II had always been a very sick child. He died of tuberculosis at the young age of twenty-one. General Ney, who had disobeyed Louis XVIII's orders to stop Napoleon, was sent to be executed.

For a few weeks, Napoleon hid at various locations throughout the country. He stayed with friends and other people who had always been loyal to him. But, on July 15, he finally surrendered to the captain of a British warship. He was taken to England, where the government tried to decide what to do with him. Some officials wanted to see Napoleon executed, but they knew that was very dangerous. Millions of people in France and around Europe were still loyal to Napoleon. Killing him could ignite yet another war.

The Mystery Of Marshal Ney

After Napoleon was defeated at Waterloo in 1815, his loyal marshal, Michel Ney, was taken back to Paris. King Louis XVIII was furious that Ney had joined Napoleon. He ordered Michel Ney to be executed. At least, that's what historians think.

But here is where the mystery starts. All of the available records suggest that Marshal Ney was executed in Paris in 1815. But for some strange reason, that's not where the story ended.

In late 1819, a mysterious stranger showed up across the ocean from France, in South Carolina. The man called himself Peter Stuart Ney. He was hired as a schoolteacher in South Carolina. He taught there for three years. Then he moved to North Carolina and taught school there, until he died in 1846.

According to legend, Peter Ney had a lot in common with Michel Ney. He had a slight foreign accent that many people thought sounded French. He had several scars, which looked as though they could have happened during war battles.

Napoleon on his way to St. Helena

Did You Know?

According to legend, Napoleon usually wore handkerchiefs around his neck when he went to battle. As the story goes, when Napoleon wore a black silk handkerchief, he always won the battle. At the Battle of Waterloo, however, he supposedly wore a white handkerchief.

Some French people who met Peter Ney when they were visiting the United States said that he resembled Michel Ney. He also sometimes referred to himself as "the marshal."

An official in North Carolina tried to look into the matter and solve the mystery. This official apparently discovered that Peter Ney's handwriting was very similar to Michel Ney's. However, that's as far as he was able to go. He never found out for sure if the two men were one and the same.

And, as the story goes, Peter Ney's own final words before dying were, "The Old Guard is defeated, now let me die." He also supposedly admitted to being Michel Ney right before he took his last breath.

Did Marshal Michel Ney escape from France and flee to the United States? We may never know for sure. However, the inscription on Peter Ney's tombstone in North Carolina may answer the question. It is said to read, "Peter Stuart Ney, a native of France and a soldier of the French Revolution under Napoleon Bonaparte."

Exile

The British finally decided to send Napoleon into exile again. This time, however, they chose a place from which he wouldn't be able to escape. Napoleon was sent to St. Helena, a volcanic island off the west coast of Africa. St. Helena is only about half the size of Elba. It is ten miles long and six miles wide. It is more than 700 miles away from the nearest land. The British used it as a stopping point for ships carrying goods and people to and from India.

Napoleon was allowed three personal officers and twelve servants. He spent his final years gardening, riding horses, and **dictating** his *memoirs*, the autobiography of his life.

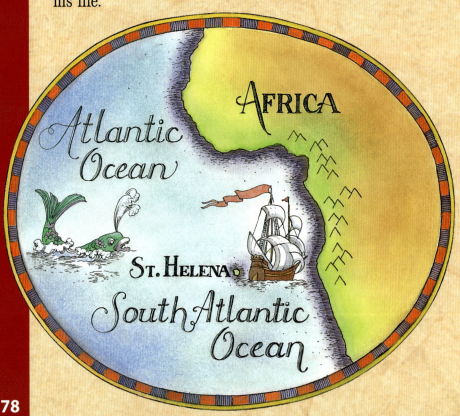

DID YOU KNOW?

St. Helena is an even smaller island than Elba, at about half the size. It is about 1,250 miles west of the coast of Africa. Napoleon traveled to St. Helena in 1815 aboard an English ship named the HMS *Northumberland*. Napoleon's final journey across the ocean on the ship took ten weeks.

When Napoleon arrived on St. Helena, the home where he was supposed to live, Longwood, was not ready. While he was waiting for Longwood to be completed, he stayed with a British family named the Balcombes. William Balcombe was one of the managers of England's East India Company. This company was in charge of the trading of goods that traveled between India, England, and the rest of Europe and Asia.

The Balcombe family consisted of Mr. and Mrs. Balcombe and their four children. Their presence greatly enhanced Napoleon's time in St. Helena. Balcombe's daughter, Betsy, who was a young teen when Napoleon arrived, was his favorite. The two became friends. Napoleon helped Betsy with her studies of the French language, since she spoke only English.

At first, Napoleon almost seemed to be enjoying his time on St. Helena. Then, in 1816, a new British governor arrived. His named was Sir Hudson Lowe. He and Napoleon didn't get along. Lowe insisted on treating Napoleon like a prisoner. Napoleon was confined to Longwood. Lowe sent an officer to Longwood to check on Napoleon twice a day. Napoleon complained about the treatment he received from Lowe and his men. But one of Napoleon's former staff members later said that the residents of Longwood were treated fairly. Whom do you believe? Maybe it depends on whose viewpoint you decide to take.

Napoleon's Death

Six years later, on May 5, 1821, Napoleon died on St. Helena. He was only 51 years old. Even today, the cause of his death is not known for certain. Four different doctors who attended to him before he died had four different opinions about what he died from. They thought it could have been liver disease, or possibly cancer. One legend says that the British men guarding him while he was a prisoner on the island poisoned Napoleon.

In 1955, a Swedish man who was an expert on poisoning reported that Napoleon's symptoms suggested that he died of arsenic poisoning. He was able to get samples of Napoleon's hair and have them tested. (Several locks of Napoleon's hair were cut off just before he died, as keepsakes for his family and loyal supporters.) Traces of arsenic were found in the samples of Napoleon's hair. However, arsenic is a natural substance on St. Helena. It is found in the soil there. Napoleon could have eaten food that had traces of arsenic, by accident. Some historians also believe that Napoleon could have committed suicide. To this day, no one knows for sure how he died.

Napoleon's body stayed on the island until 1840, when it was brought back to France. It lies in a grand tomb under a big dome in a building in Paris. The famous building is called Les Invalides (layz an•vah•**leed**) and is also home to a large war museum.

Napoleon's remains receive a blessing.

The Legacy of Napoleon

So what do you think? How should history judge Napoleon Bonaparte? Some people think he was a political genius. Others say he was the greatest military leader of all time. Still others say that everything he did revolved around his hunger for power. Was he evil, or just ambitious?

If you are having trouble answering these questions, you are not alone. They are the same questions that people have been asking since Napoleon's rise to power more than 200 years ago. Perhaps the best answer is that Napoleon Bonaparte was all of these things and much more.

Did You Know?

Napoleon was so famous that he had some recipes named after him! At least historians think they were probably named after him.

A Napoleon is a dessert made of layers of flaky puff pastry and cream, and then topped with icing. Napoleons are usually made in small, rectangular shapes, just large enough for one serving.

One legend says that a Danish pastry chef invented the dessert when Bonaparte was visiting Denmark. The chef named the dessert after Napoleon to honor him. Another legend says that the French invented the dessert. It was named after Napoleon simply because it was his favorite. As the story goes, he ate too many of them the night before the Battle of Waterloo. Some say that is why he lost! However, other people believe that the name Napoleon is actually a confusion of the name Neapolitan, which is an Italian dessert that is very similar to the Napoleon.

Chicken Marengo is another dish that some historians believe has a connection to Napoleon. Apparently, after defeating the Austrians at the Battle of Marengo, he was very hungry! However, his cook, named Dunand, was running out of ingredients, so he had to use whatever he had left and whatever he could find locally. The result was Chicken Marengo, a dish made with chicken, butter, garlic, onions, wine, mushrooms, and toast.

Glossary

abolished (uh·**bol**·isht) got rid of

ally (**al**·eye) a person or country joined with another in order to meet common goals

ambitious (am·**bish**·uhs) having a strong desire to succeed

bombard (bom·**bard**) to attack continuously with guns or bombs

dictating (**dik**·tay·ting) saying aloud to another person who writes down the words

dictator (**dik**·tay·tuhr) a person who has absolute authority to rule a country

disband (dis·**band**) to break up

eliminate (i·**lim**·uh·nayt) to get rid of

guillotine (**gil**·uh·teen) a French invention for beheading people who have broken the law

heir (air) a person who has the right to someone's property or title after the death of its owner

morale (muh·**ral**) a mental attitude that has to do with happiness and high self-confidence

negotiate (ni·**goh**·shee·ayt) to discuss terms and reach an agreement, like in business

outmaneuvered (**out**·muh·**noo**·vuhrd) got the better of someone by making a clever move

persistent (puhr·**sis**·tuhnt) not giving up, especially in the face of difficulties

polls (pohlz) where citizens go to cast a vote

prestigious (pres·**tee**·juhs) having respect or importance in the opinion of others

reclaim (ri·**klaym**) to take back

revolution (rev·uh·**loo**·shuhn) a movement to get rid of one government and replace it with another

solemn (**sol**·uhm) gloomy or sad

successor (suhk·**ses**·uhr) someone who follows someone else

viceroy (**vys**·roy) a person who rules a country that is ruled by another country

yearned (yurnd) wanted very badly

INDEX

Ajaccio, 2–3

Amiens, Treaty of, 41

Antoinette, Marie, 11, 14, 59

Appert, Nicholas, 22

Austerlitz, Battle of, 50

Austria, 17, 23, 27–28, 41–42, 47, 49–50, 57–58, 60, 67

Bastille, 12–13

Beauharnais, Josephine, de, 21–23, 29–30, 45–47, 53–56, 59–60, 70

Blücher, Gebhard von, 73

Buonaparte, Carlo, 4–5, 8

Buonaparte, Jerome, 51

Buonaparte, Joseph, 3, 8, 44, 52

Buonaparte, Letizia, 4–5

Buonaparte, Louis, 51

Buonaparte, Lucien, 37, 44

Carteaux, General, 18

Code Napoleon, 1, 40

Continental System, 51

Corsica, 2–3, 5, 8, 15–16

Dugommier, General, 18

Egypt, 29–35, 41

Elba, 70, 72, 78–79

England, 12, 15, 17, 29, 40-42, 44, 47, 49–52, 73–74, 76, 79

hieroglyphics, 32

Iberian Peninsula, 52

Italy, 2, 23–25, 28–29, 31, 34, 40, 51, 70

Louis XVI, 9–12, 14, 16, 40, 59, 71

Louis XVIII, 71–72, 76

Louisiana Purchase, 42

Louvre, 28–29

Marengo, 41, 74, 82

Marie Louise, 57–60, 70

Napoleon II, 60, 70, 75–76

Nelson, Admiral Horatio, 33, 47–49

Ney, General Michel, 72, 76–77

Ney, Peter, 77

Notre Dame, 45

Paoli, Pasquale, 5, 15

Portugal, 51–52

Prussia, 17, 47, 67

Revolutionary calendar, 49

Robespierre, Maximilien, 19–20

Rosetta Stone, 31–32

Russia, 47, 60–64, 66–68

Spain, 17, 30, 47–48, 52, 67

Sphinx, 35

St. Helena, 77–80

Toulon, 17–20, 31

Trafalgar, 47–50

United States, 13, 39, 42–44, 70, 77

Waterloo, 22, 69, 73–75, 77, 82

Wellesley, Arthur, 67, 73–74

Wellington, Duke of, 73

Wurmser, Count Dagobart Sigismund von, 27–28